Beans, Nuts, and Oils

D.H. Dilkes

Enslow Elementary
an imprint of

Enslow Publishers, Inc.
40 Industrial Road
Box 398
Berkeley Heights, NJ 07922
USA

http://www.enslow.com

For my girls: Nicole, Jocelynn, and Devynn

Enslow Elementary, an imprint of Enslow Publishers, Inc.
Enslow Elementary® is a registered trademark of Enslow Publishers, Inc.

Library of Congress Cataloging-in-Publication Data

Dilkes, D.H.
  Beans, nuts, and oils / D.H. Dilkes.
    p. cm. — (All about good foods we eat)
  Includes bibliographical references and index.
  Summary: "Introduces beans, nuts, and oils to pre-readers using repetition of words and short, simple sentences with photos and illustrations to enhance the text"—Provided by publisher.
  ISBN 978-0-7660-3928-5
  1. Beans—Juvenile literature. 2. Nuts—Juvenile literature. 3. Oils and fats, Edible—Juvenile literature. I. Title.
  TX558.B4D55 2012
  664'.3—dc23   2011015670

Paperback ISBN 978-1-59845-256-3

Printed in the United States of America
052011 Lake Book Manufacturing, Inc., Melrose Park, IL

10 9 8 7 6 5 4 3 2 1

To Our Readers: We have done our best to make sure all Internet Addresses in this book were active and appropriate when we went to press. However, the author and the publisher have no control over and assume no liability for the material available on those Internet sites or on other Web sites they may link to. Any comments or suggestions can be sent by e-mail to comments@enslow.com or to the address on the back cover.

Enslow Publishers, Inc., is committed to printing our books on recycled paper. The paper in every book contains 10% to 30% post-consumer waste (PCW). The cover board on the outside of each book contains 100% PCW. Our goal is to do our part to help young people and the environment too!

Photo Credits: Shutterstock.com

Cover Photo: Shutterstock.com

Note to Parents and Teachers
Help pre-readers get a jumpstart on reading. These lively stories introduce simple concepts with repetition of words and short simple sentences. Photos and illustrations fill the pages with color and effectively enhance the text. Free Educator Guides are available for this series at www.enslow.com. Search for the *All About Good Foods We Eat* series name.

Warning: The foods in this book may contain ingredients to which people may be allergic, such as peanuts and milk.

Contents

Words to Know

falafel

olive oil

walnut

Mom likes cereal bars with nuts.

They are part of her breakfast.

Walnuts are in these muffins.

They are part of my breakfast.

There is peanut butter on my sandwich.

I eat it for lunch.

I have nuts on my plate.

They are part of my healthy lunch.

My sister
likes falafel
for lunch.

It is made
with beans.

My family cooks with olive oil. It helps us make dinner.

I like lima beans with dinner.

I mix them with veggies.

I am eating walnuts.

They are a good snack.

I am holding peanuts.

I will eat them for a snack.

Happy birthday to my brother!

He likes almond cake for dessert.

Read More

Burstein, John. *Marvelous Meats and More*. New York: Crabtree Pub., 2010.

Leedy, Loren. *The Edible Pyramid: Good Eating Every Day*. New York: Holiday House, 2007.

Web Sites

PBS Kids: *Sid the Science Kid* Mix it Up
<http://pbskids.org/sid/mixitup.html>
Help Sid create a balanced meal!

Smallstep Kids: MyPyramid Blast Off
<http://teamnutrition.usda.gov/Resources/game/BlastOff_Game.html>
A fun game that teaches about the food pyramid.

Index

Guided Reading Level: **D**
Guided Reading Leveling System is based on the guidelines recommended by Fountas and Pinnell.

Word Count: 112